 Cover Art And Work By Terry Urban

ISBN-13:978-1517007287

ISBN-10:1517007283

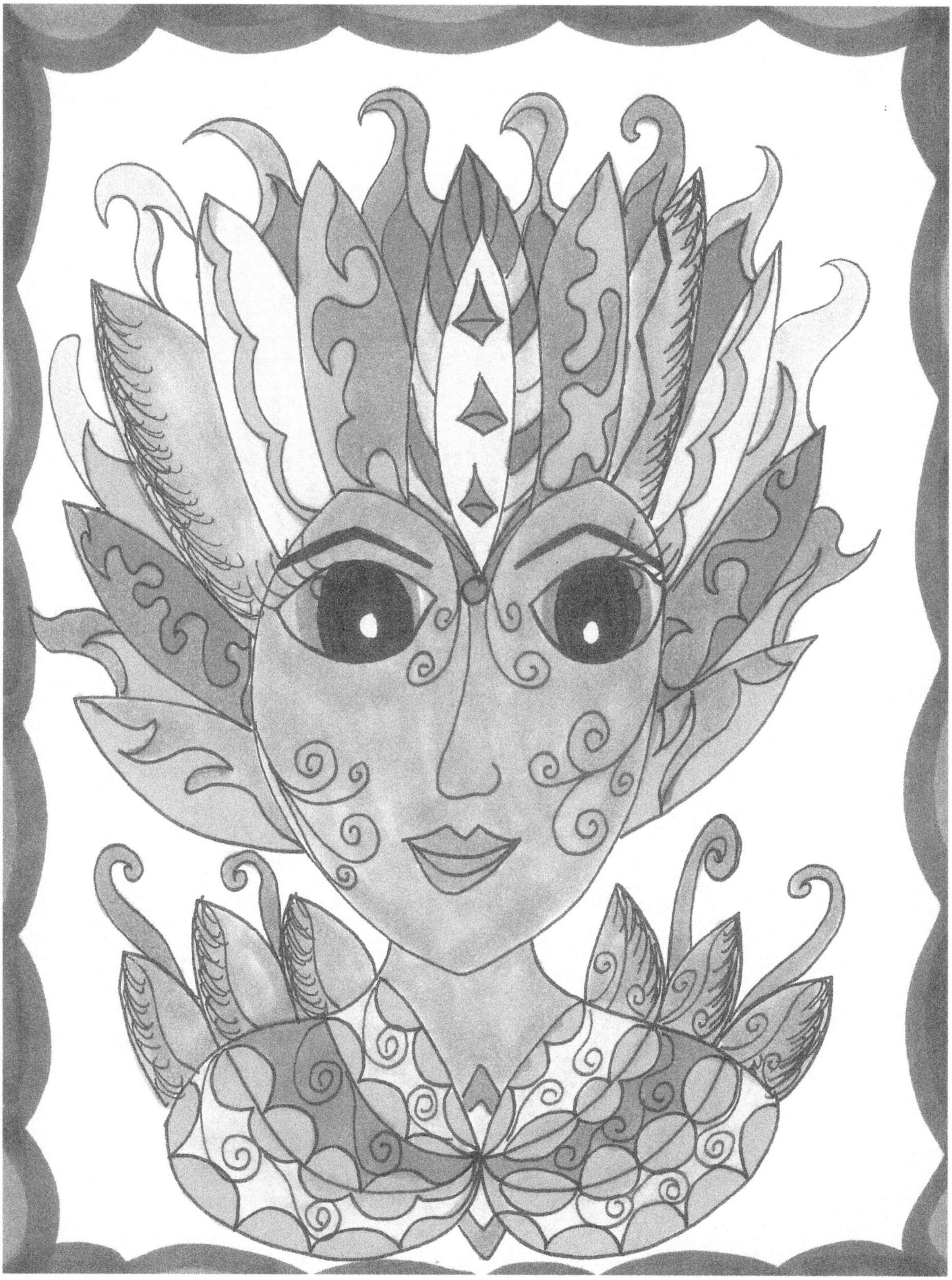

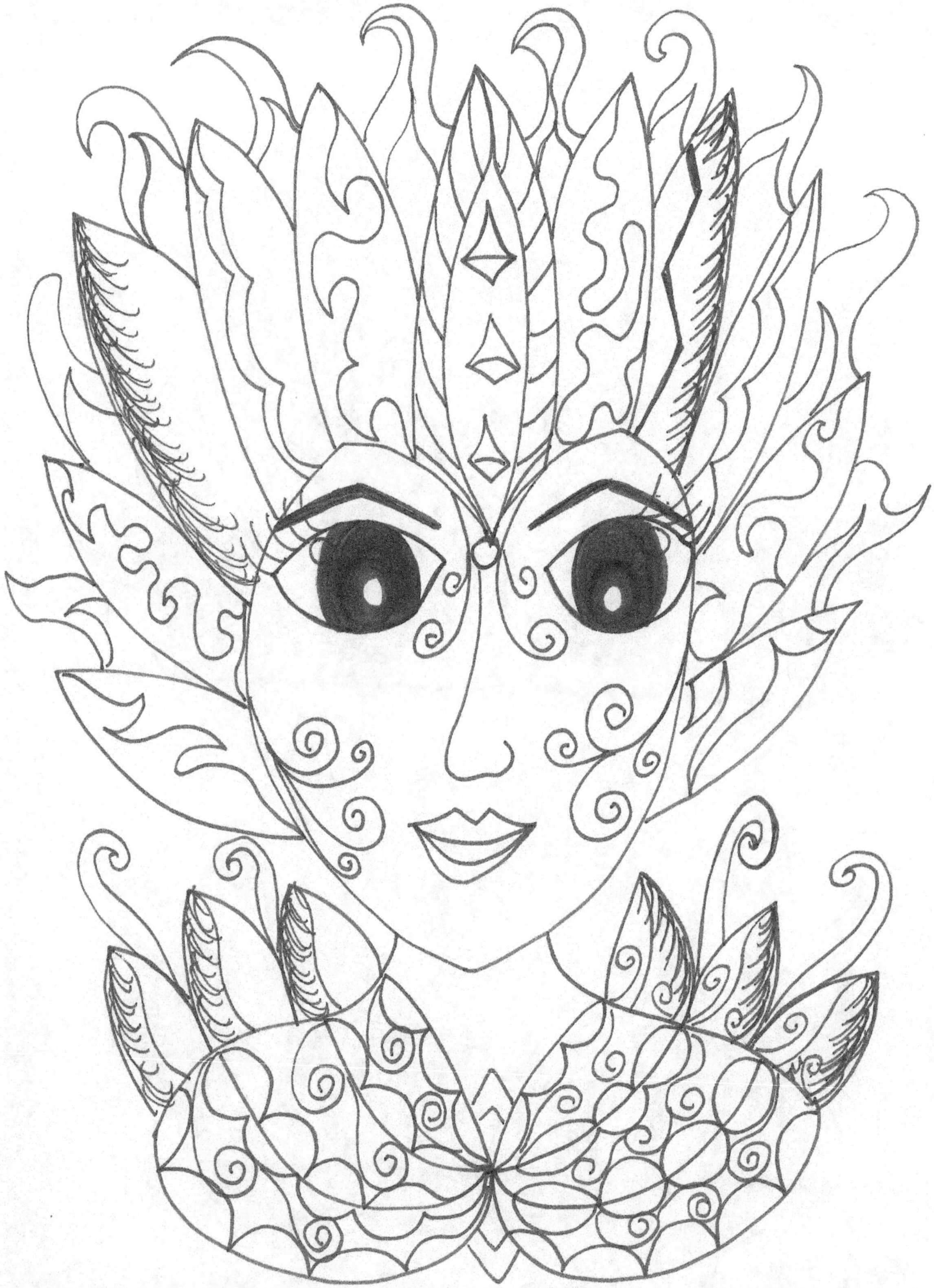

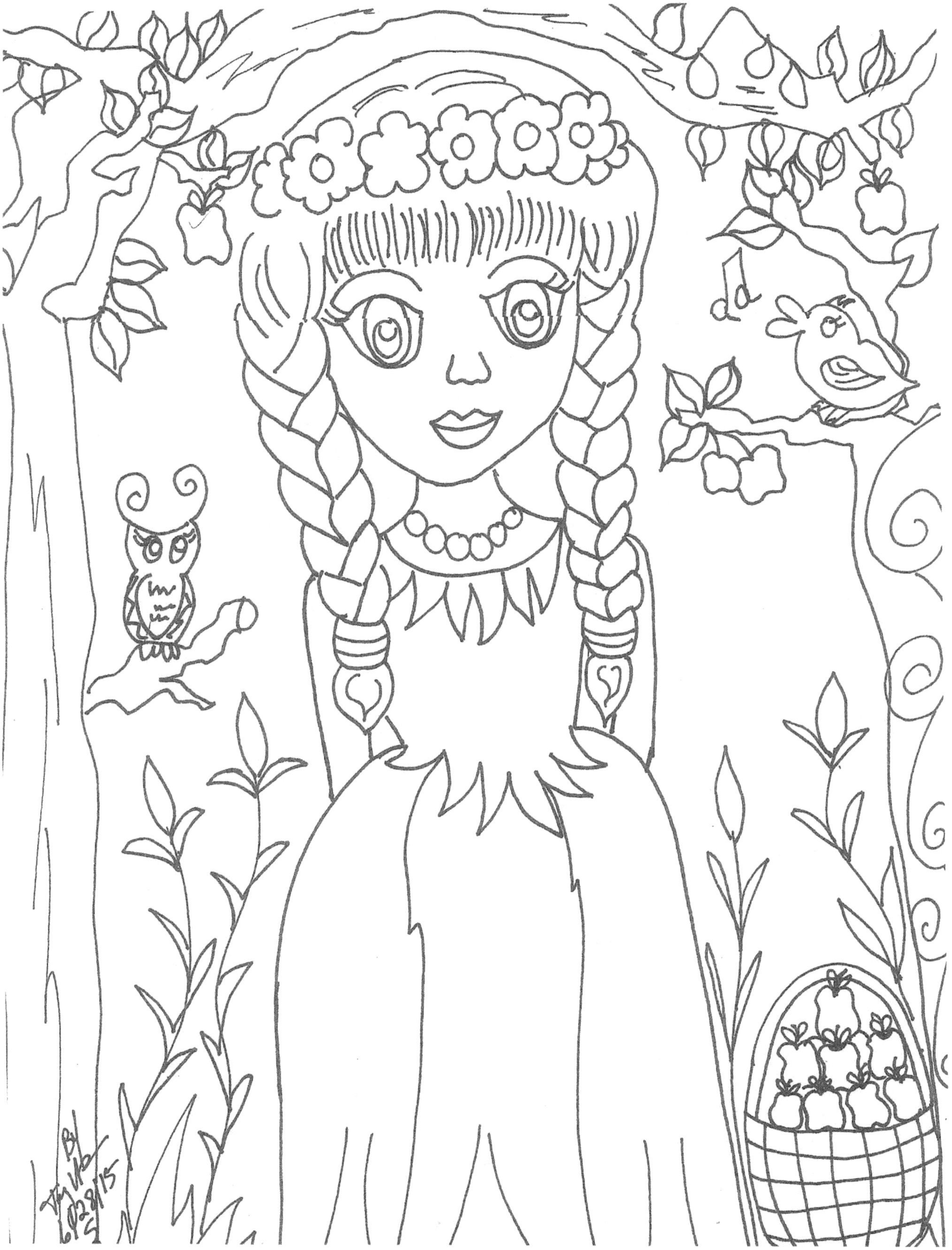
By
6/28/15

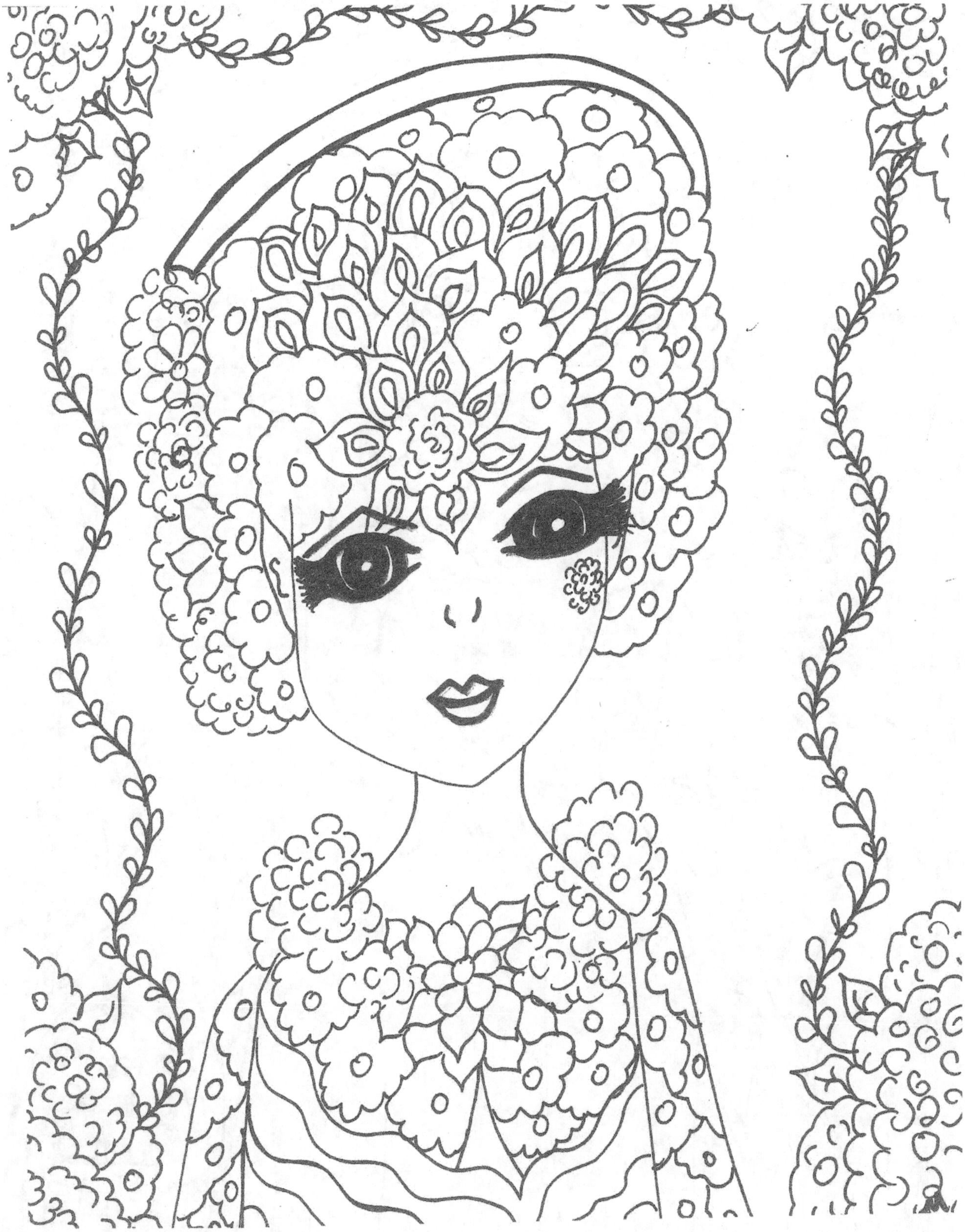

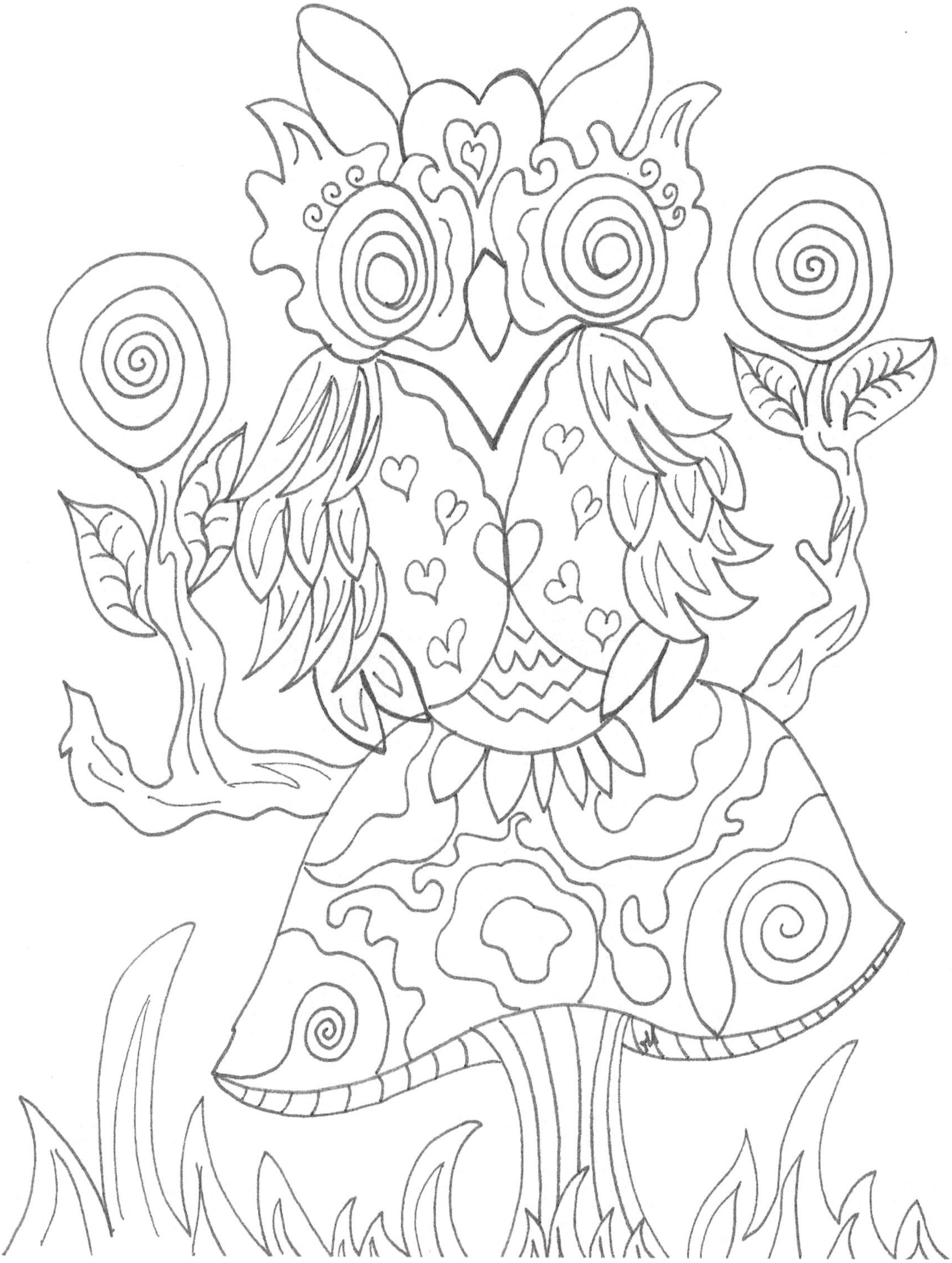

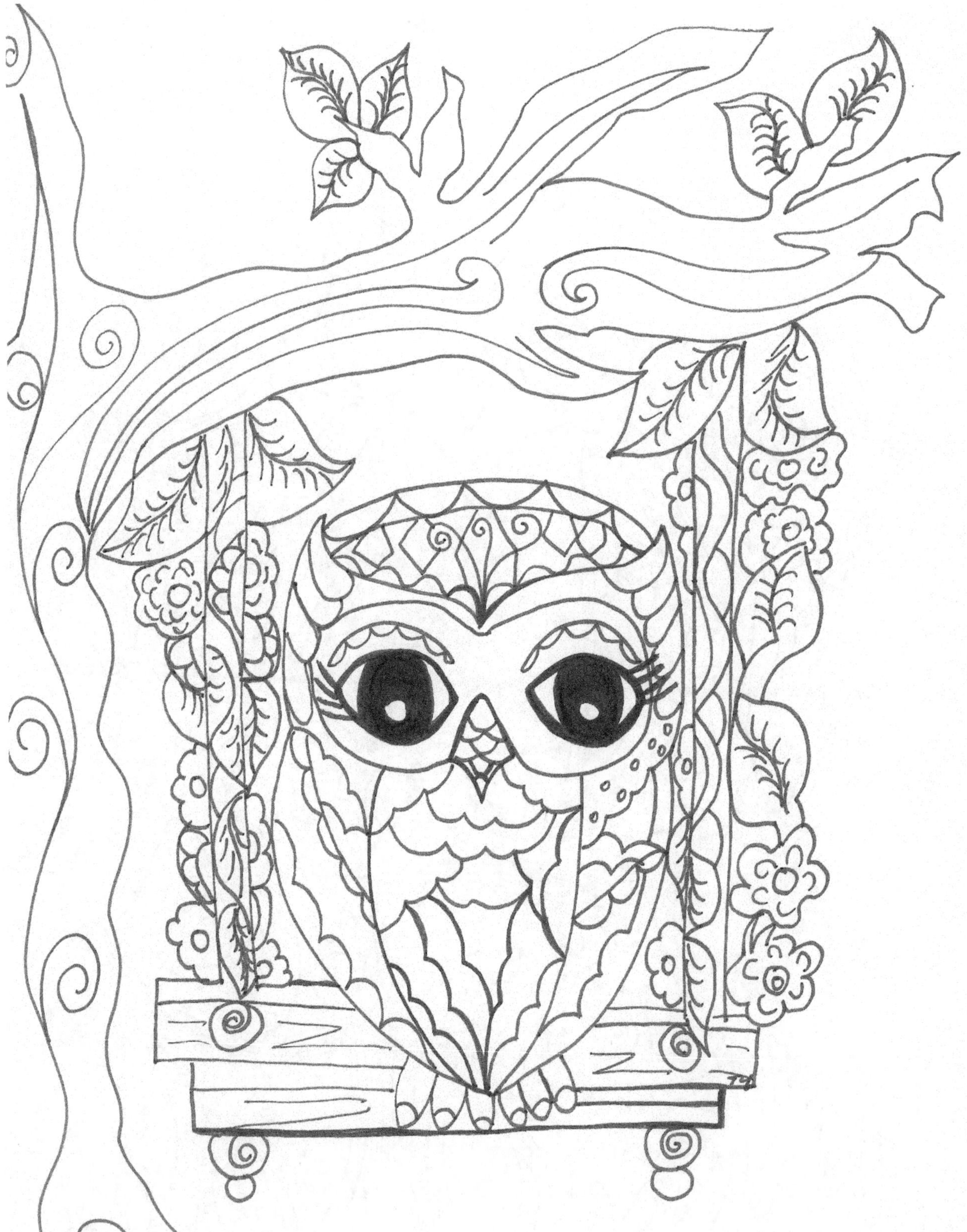

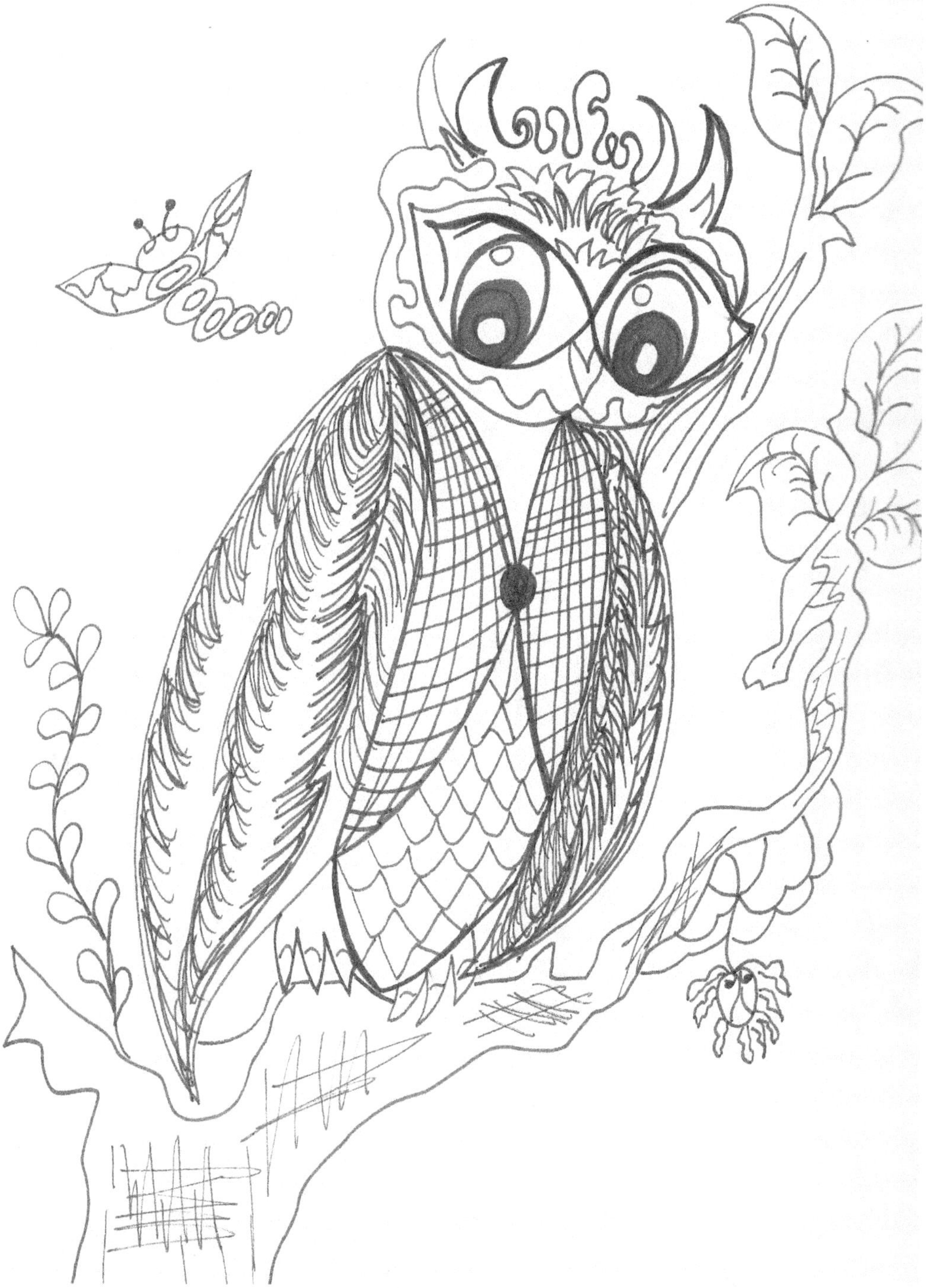

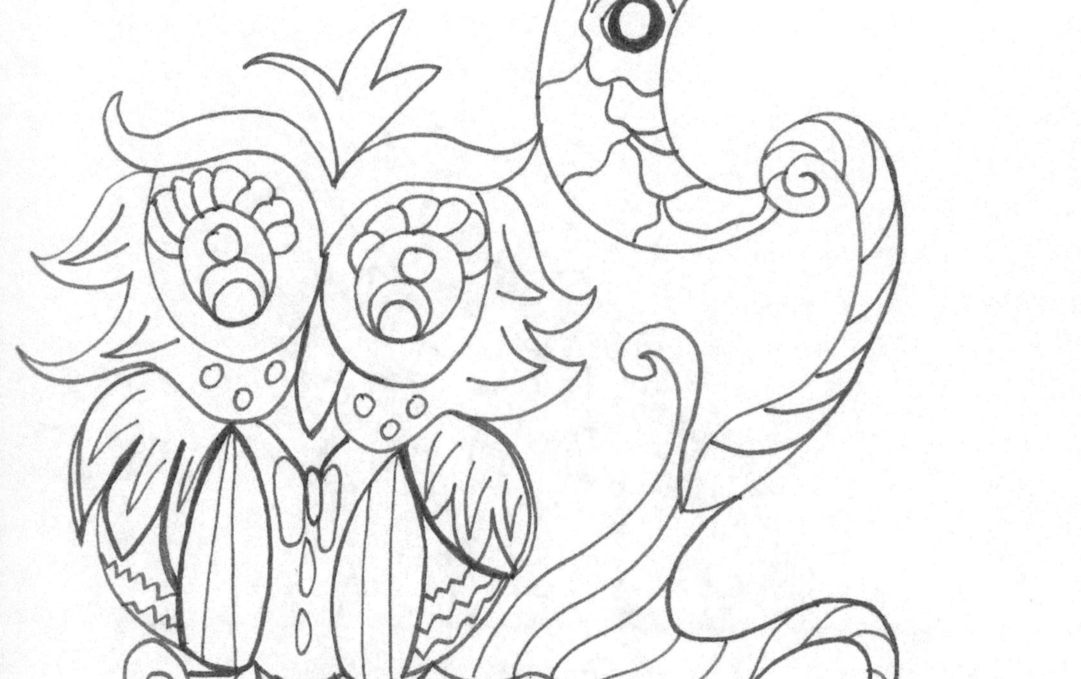

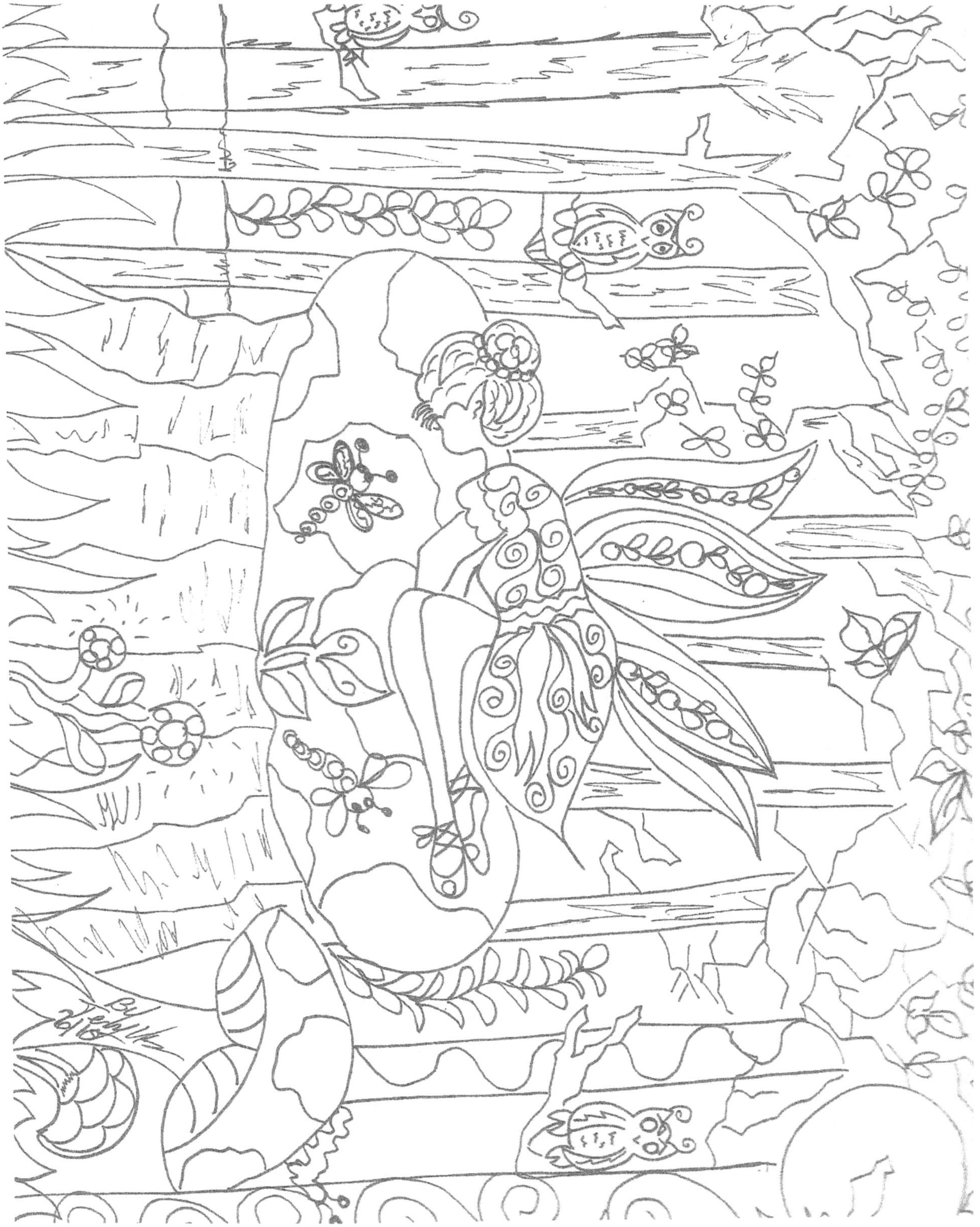

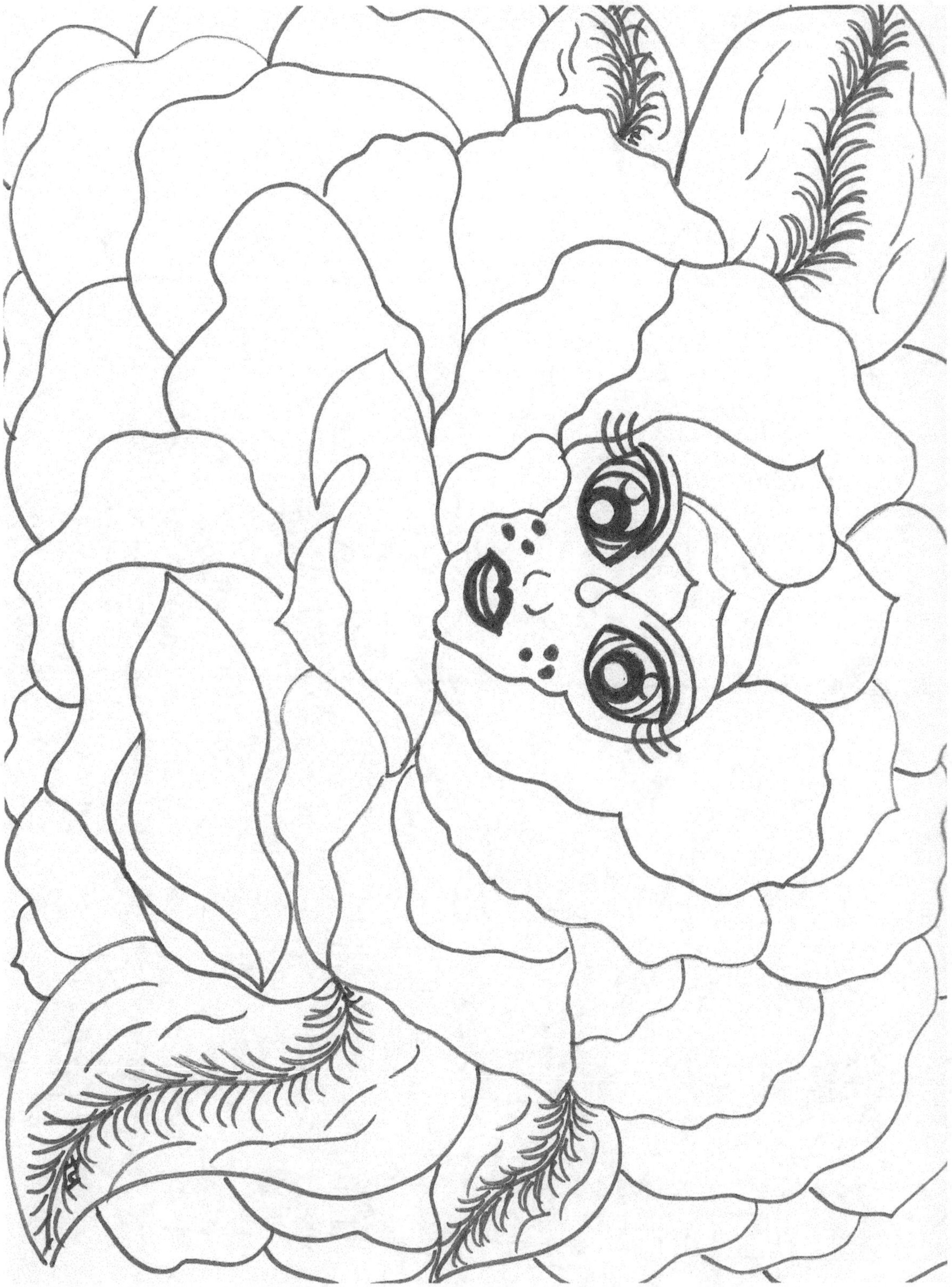

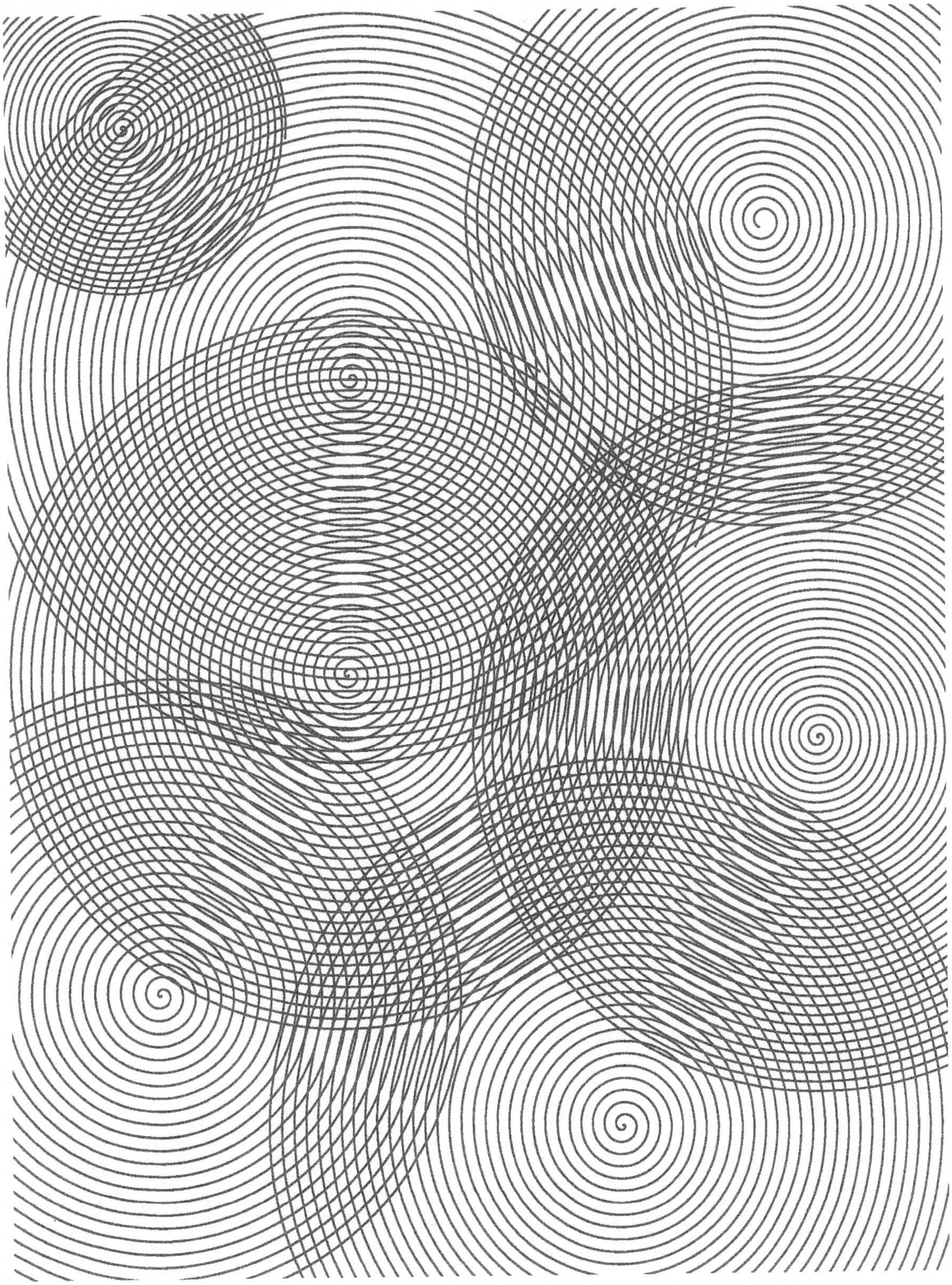

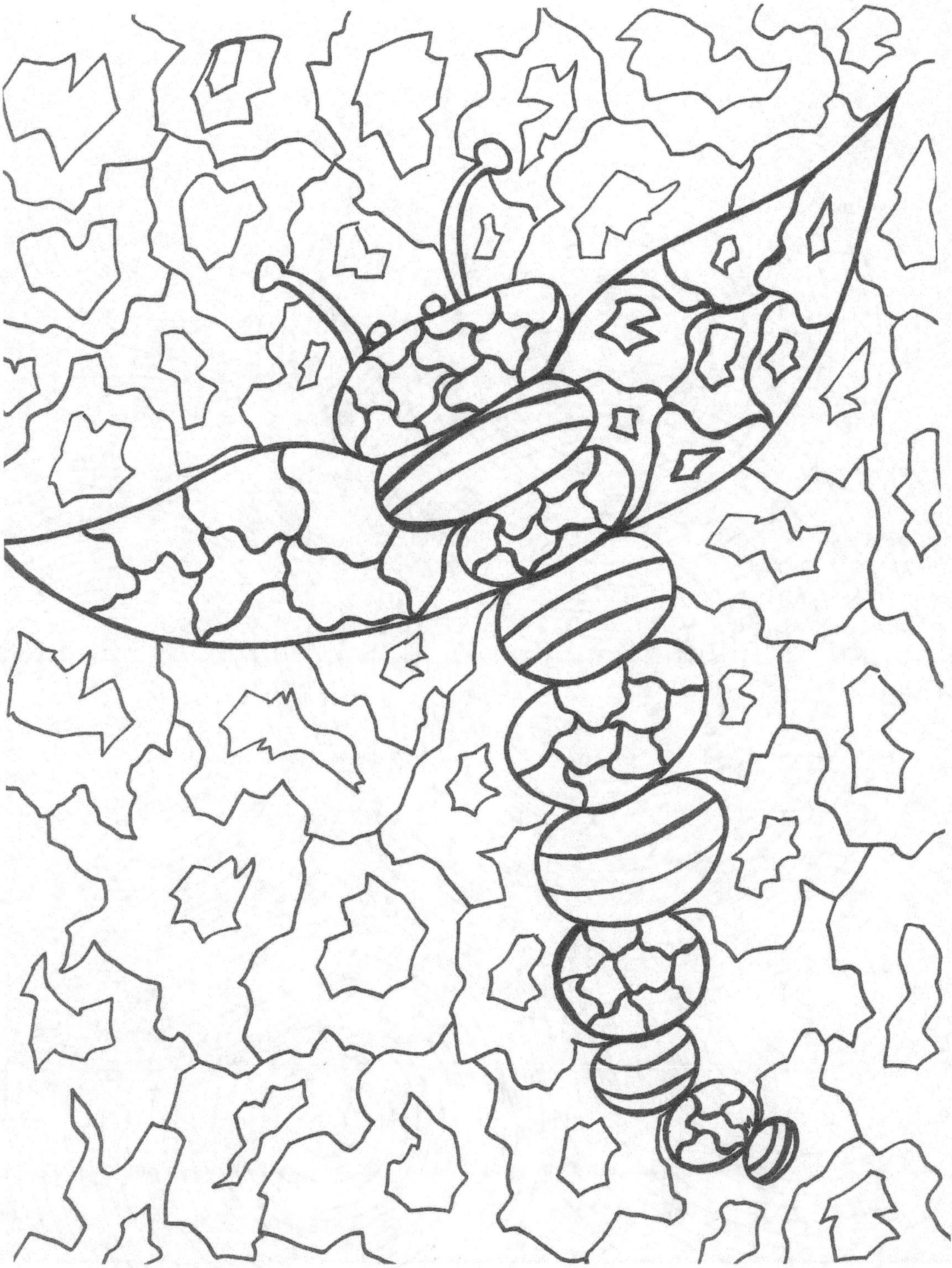

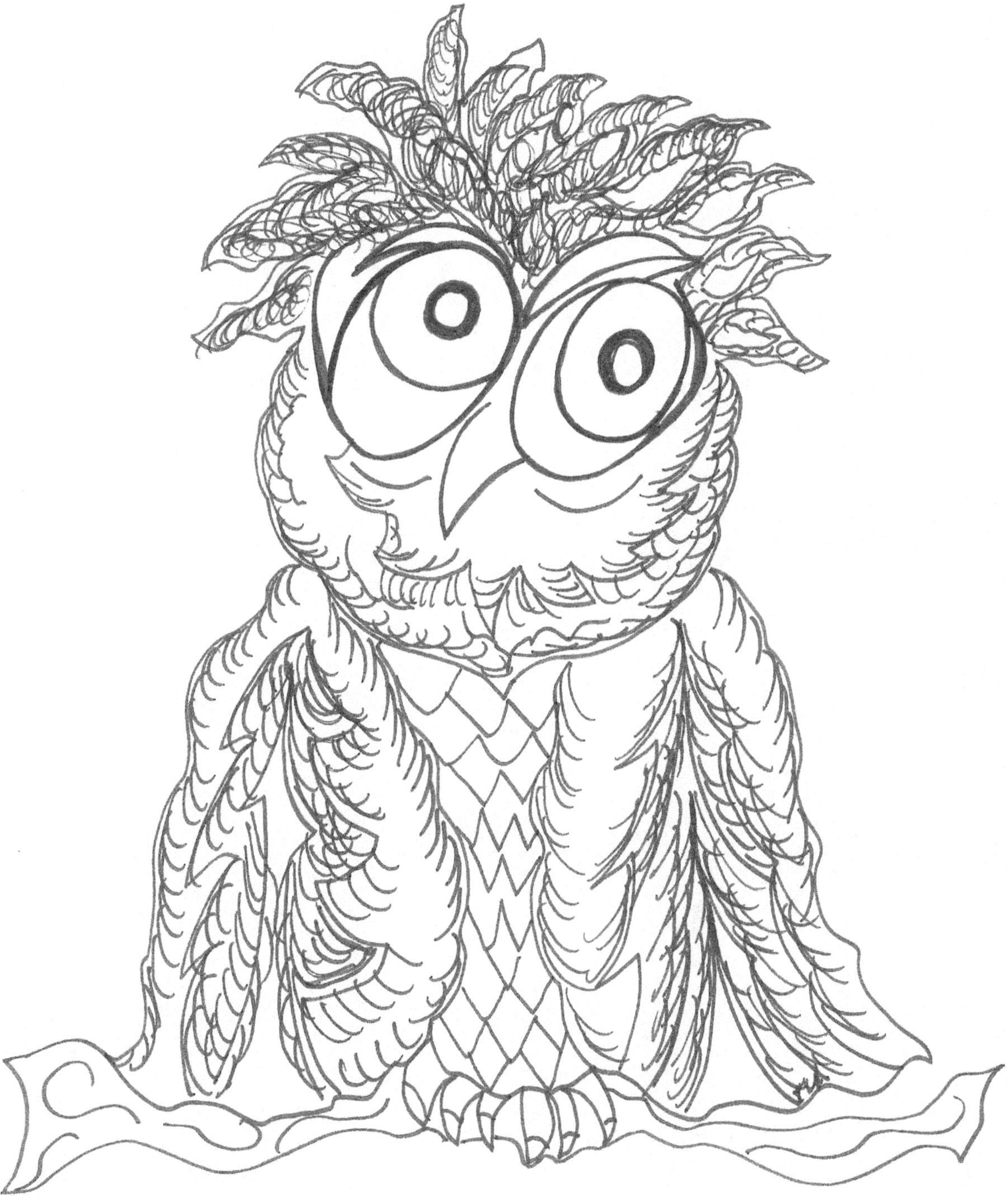

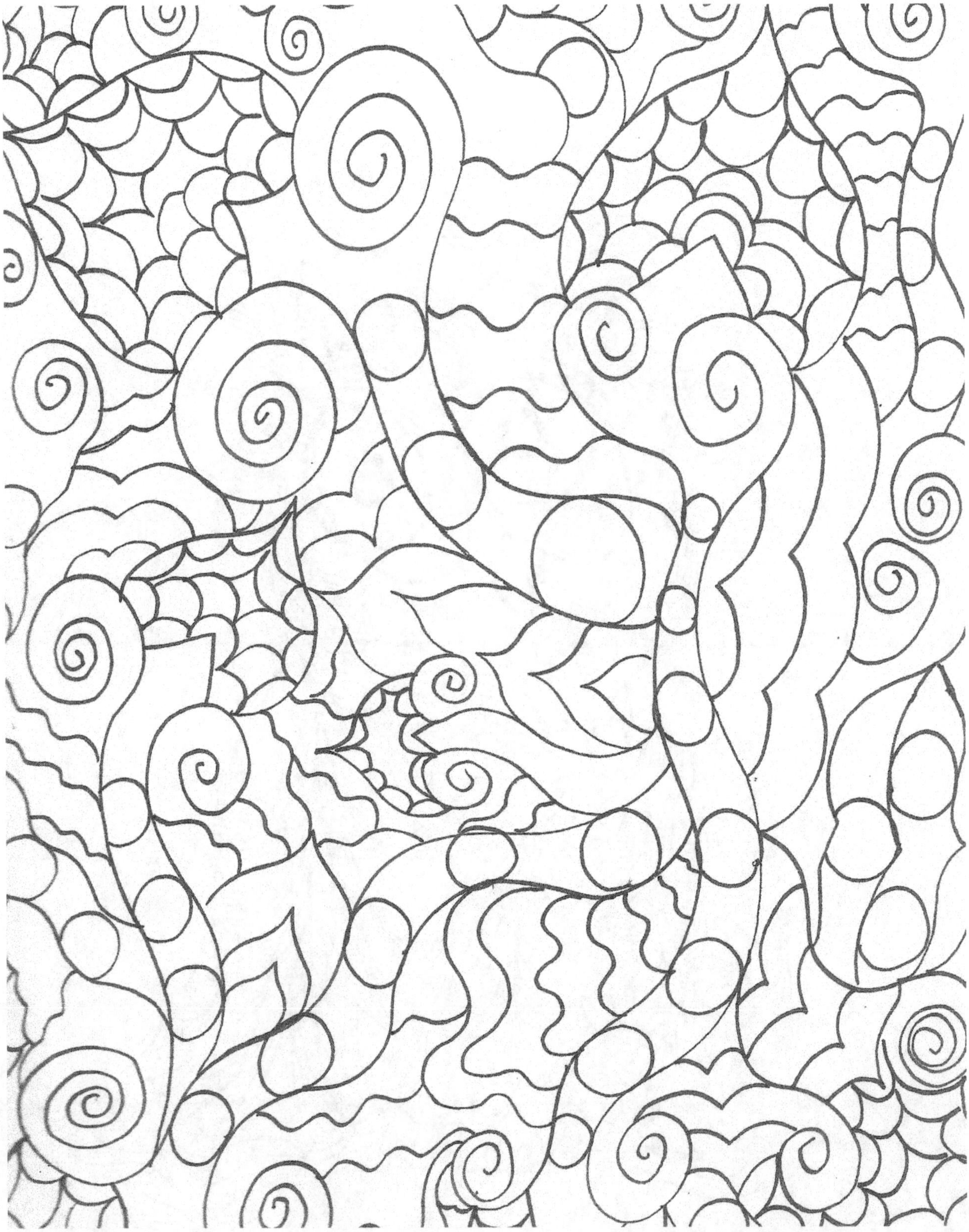

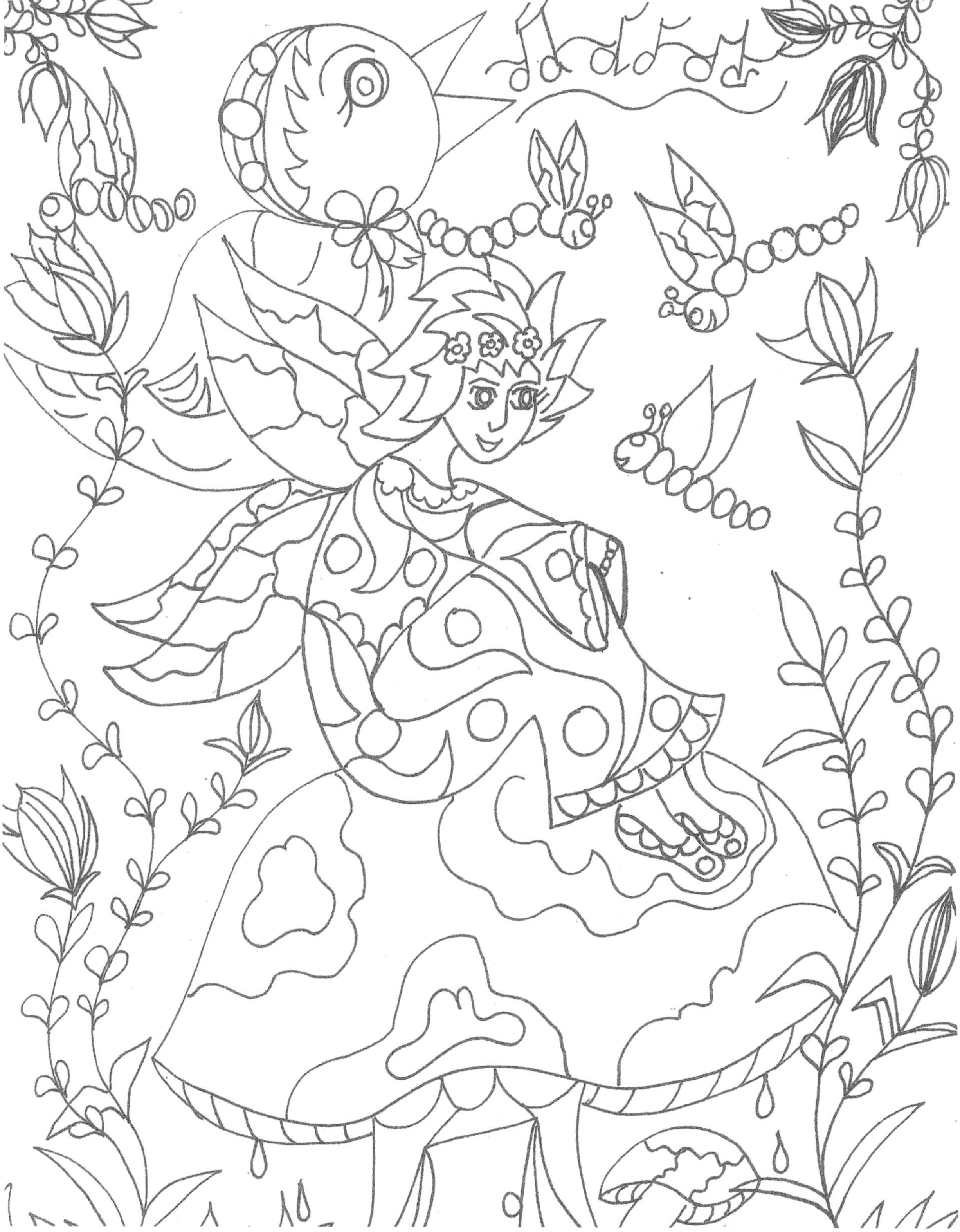

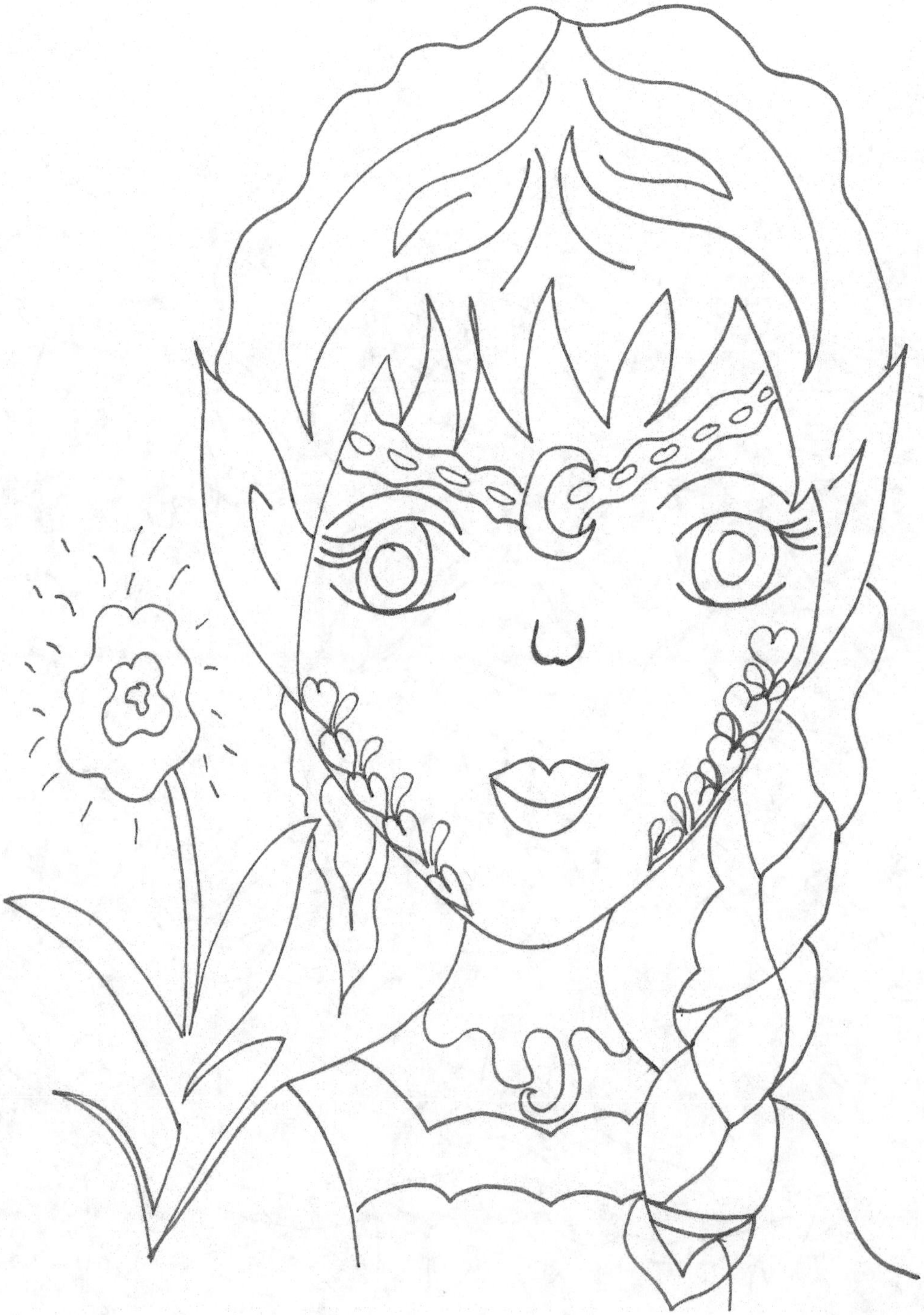

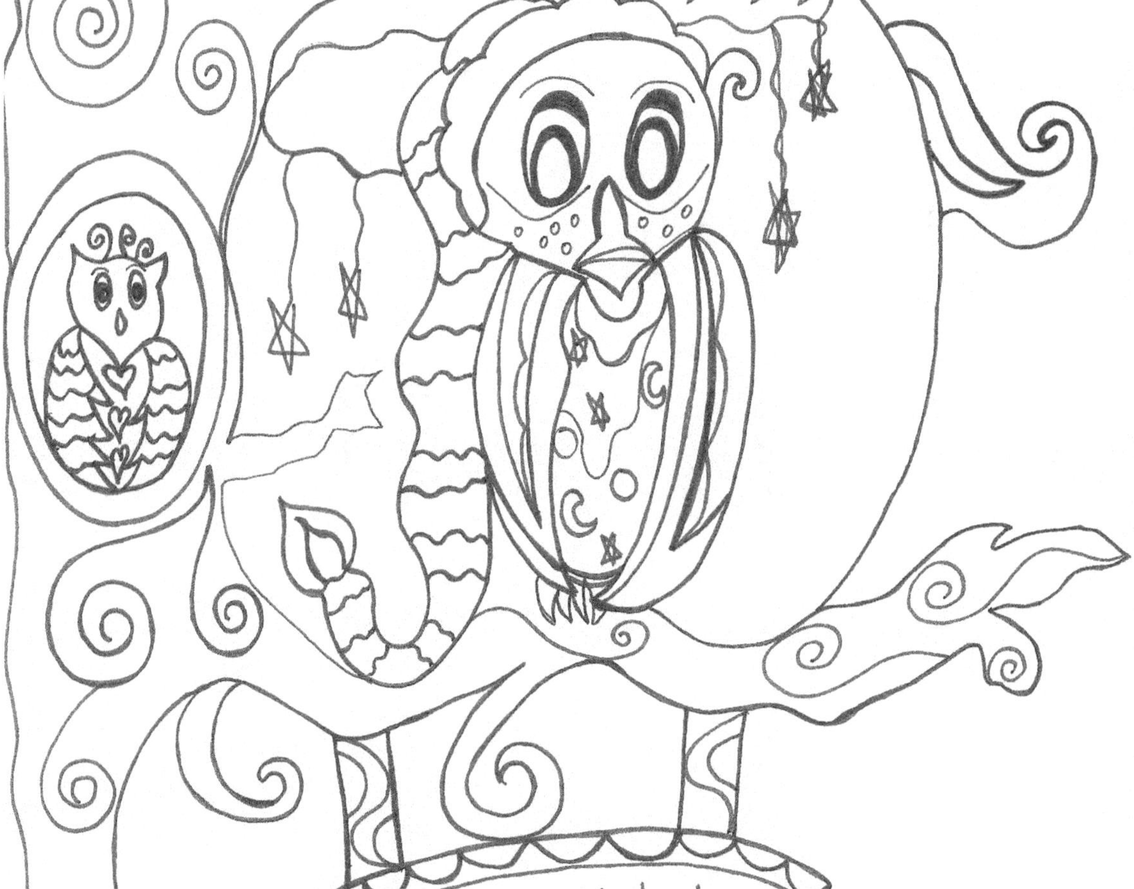
Good Night
Mr Moon

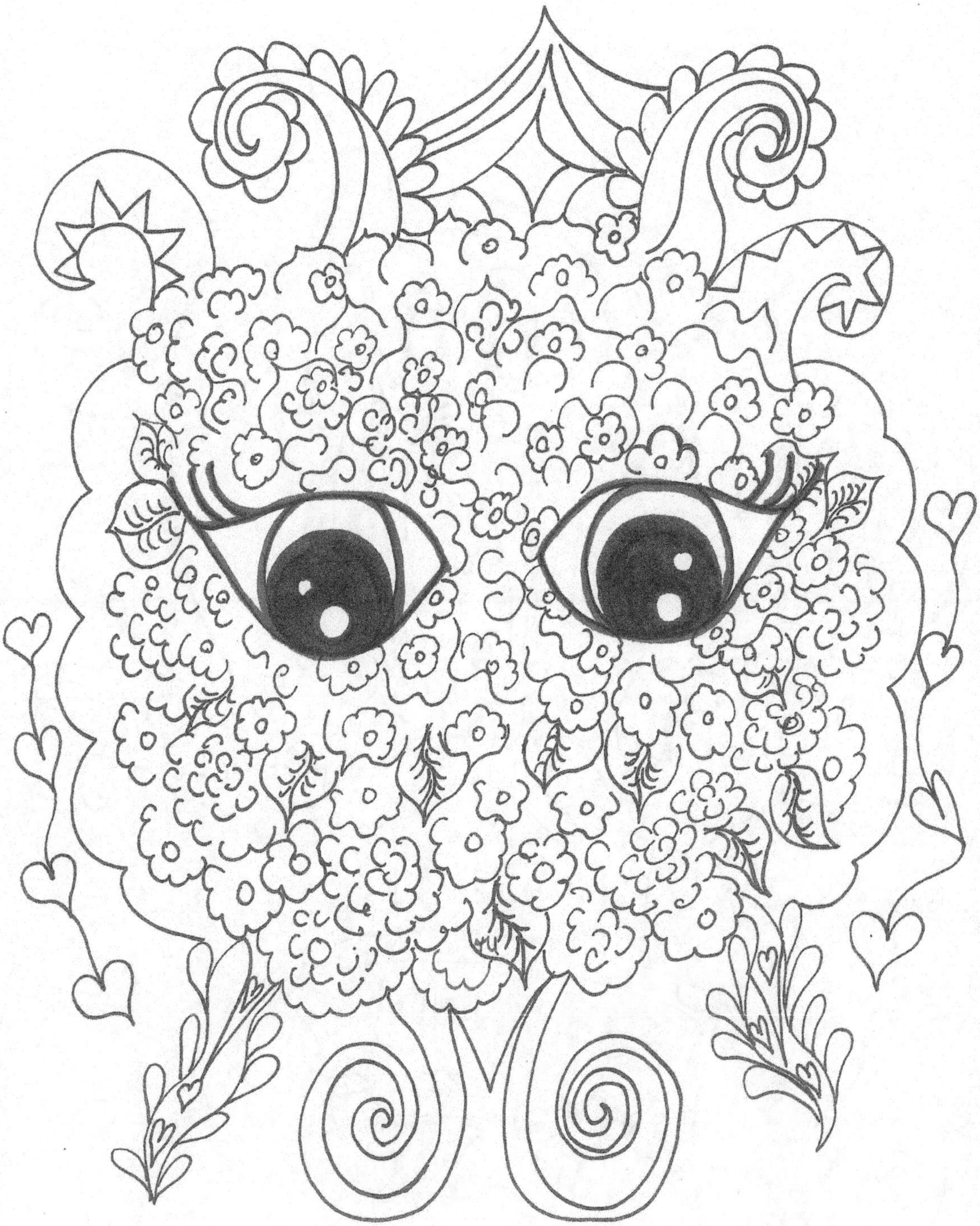

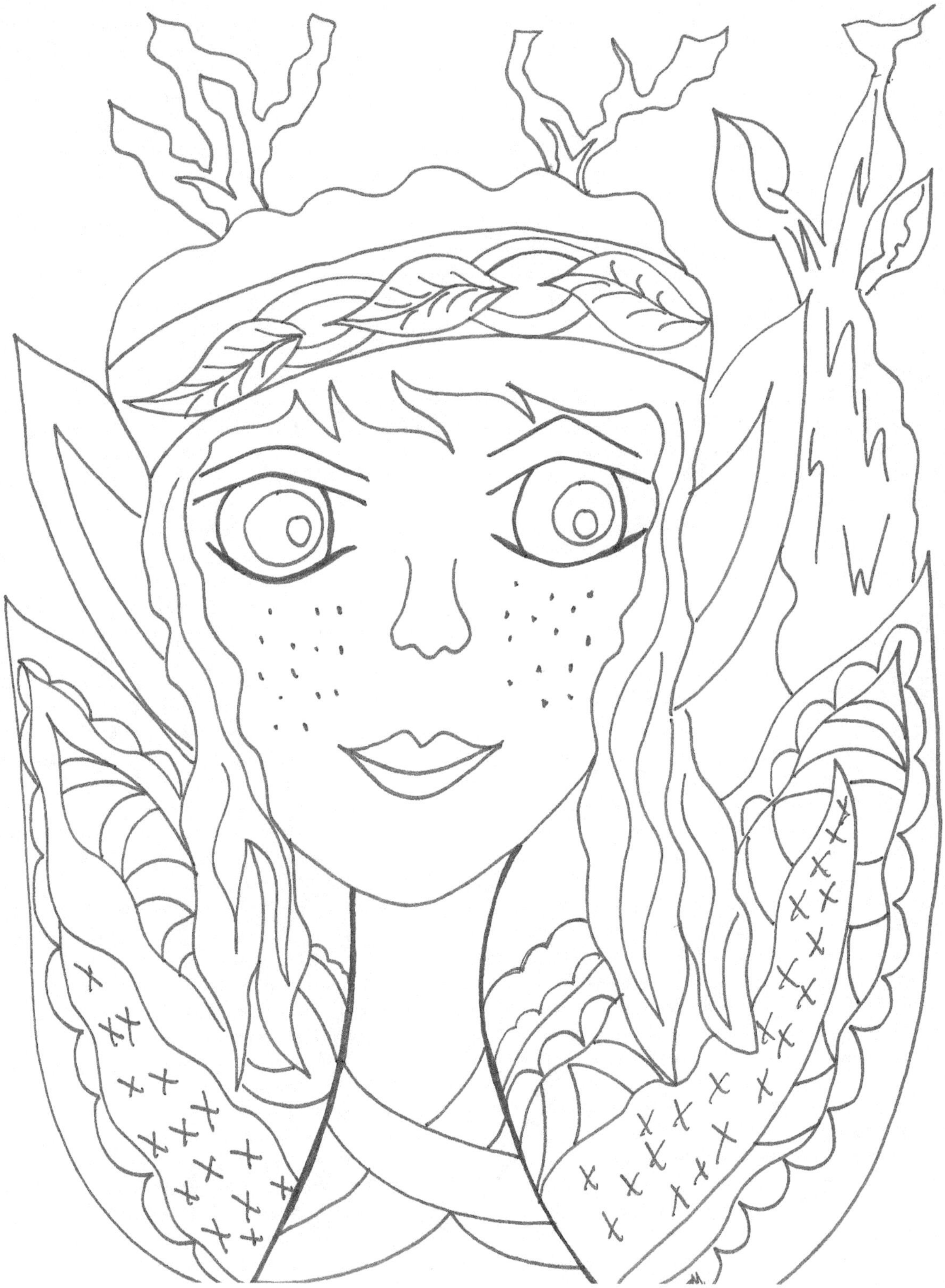

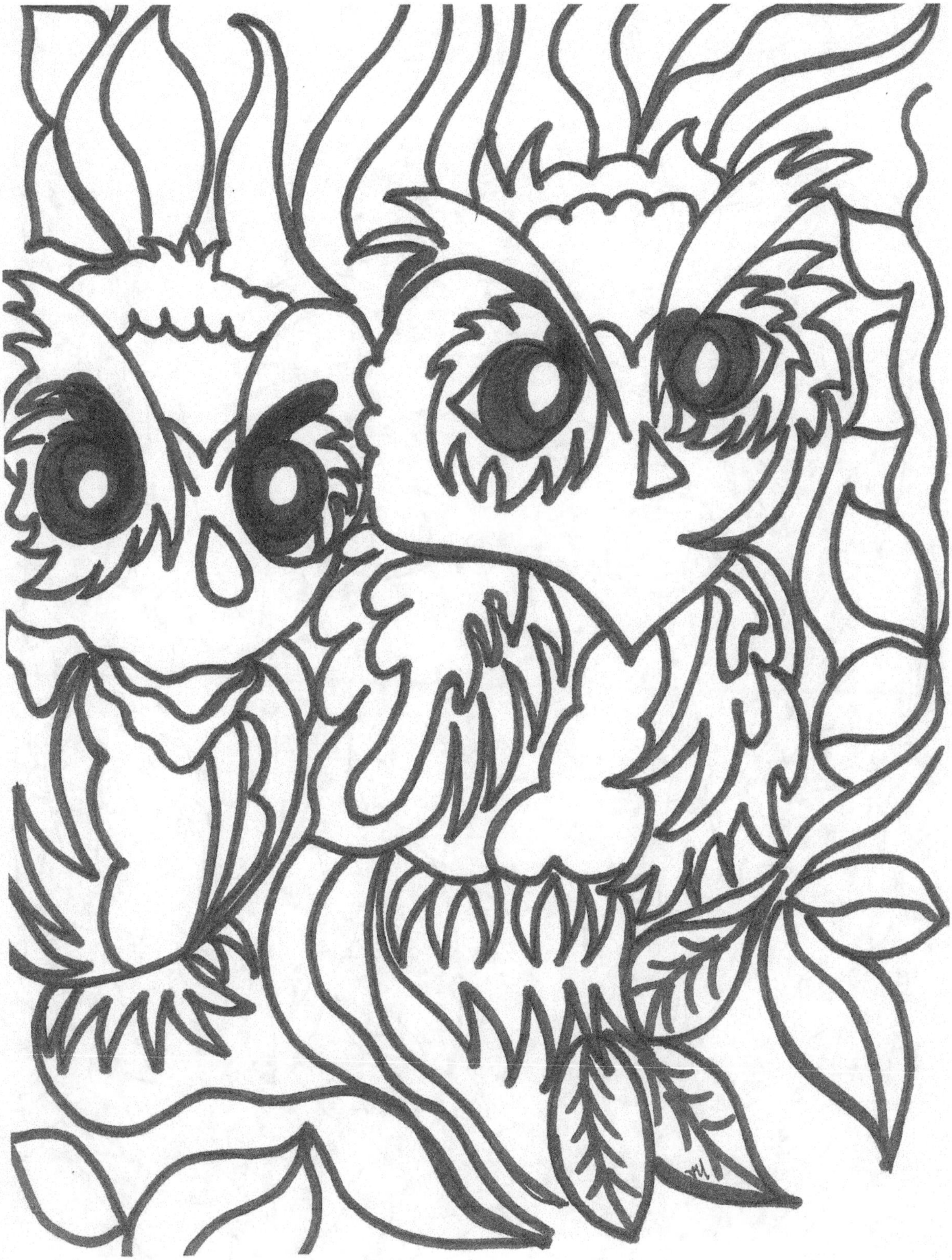

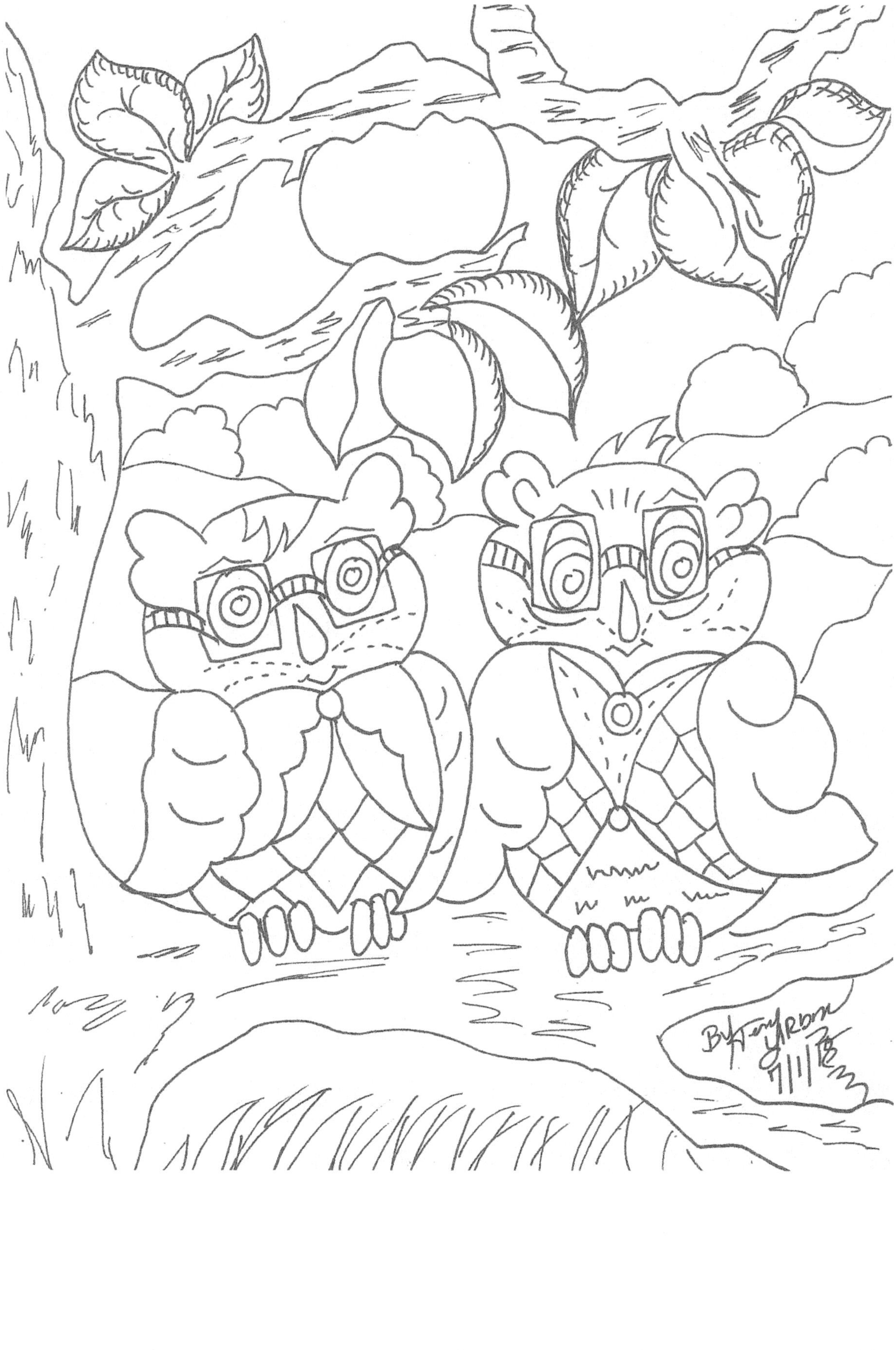

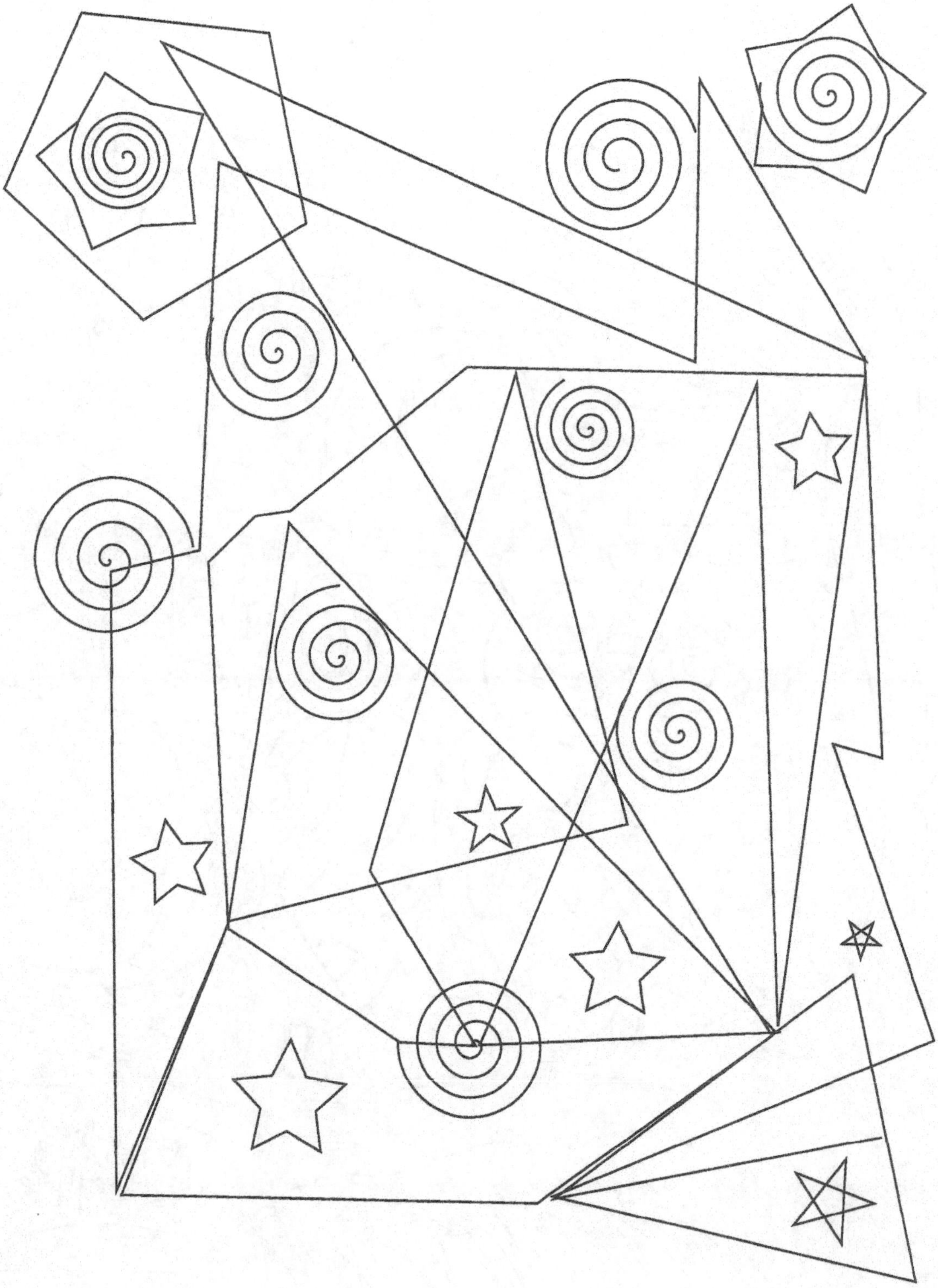

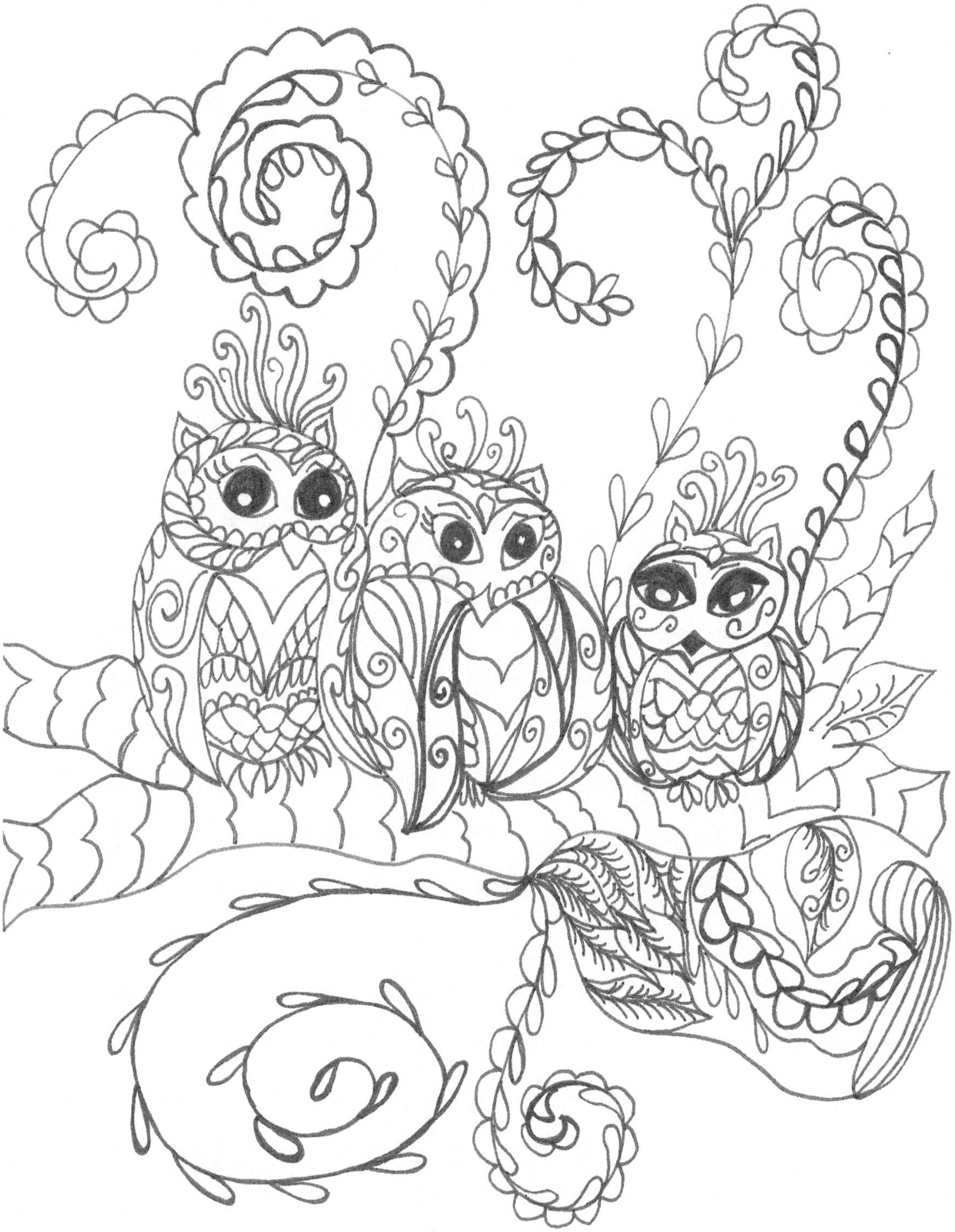

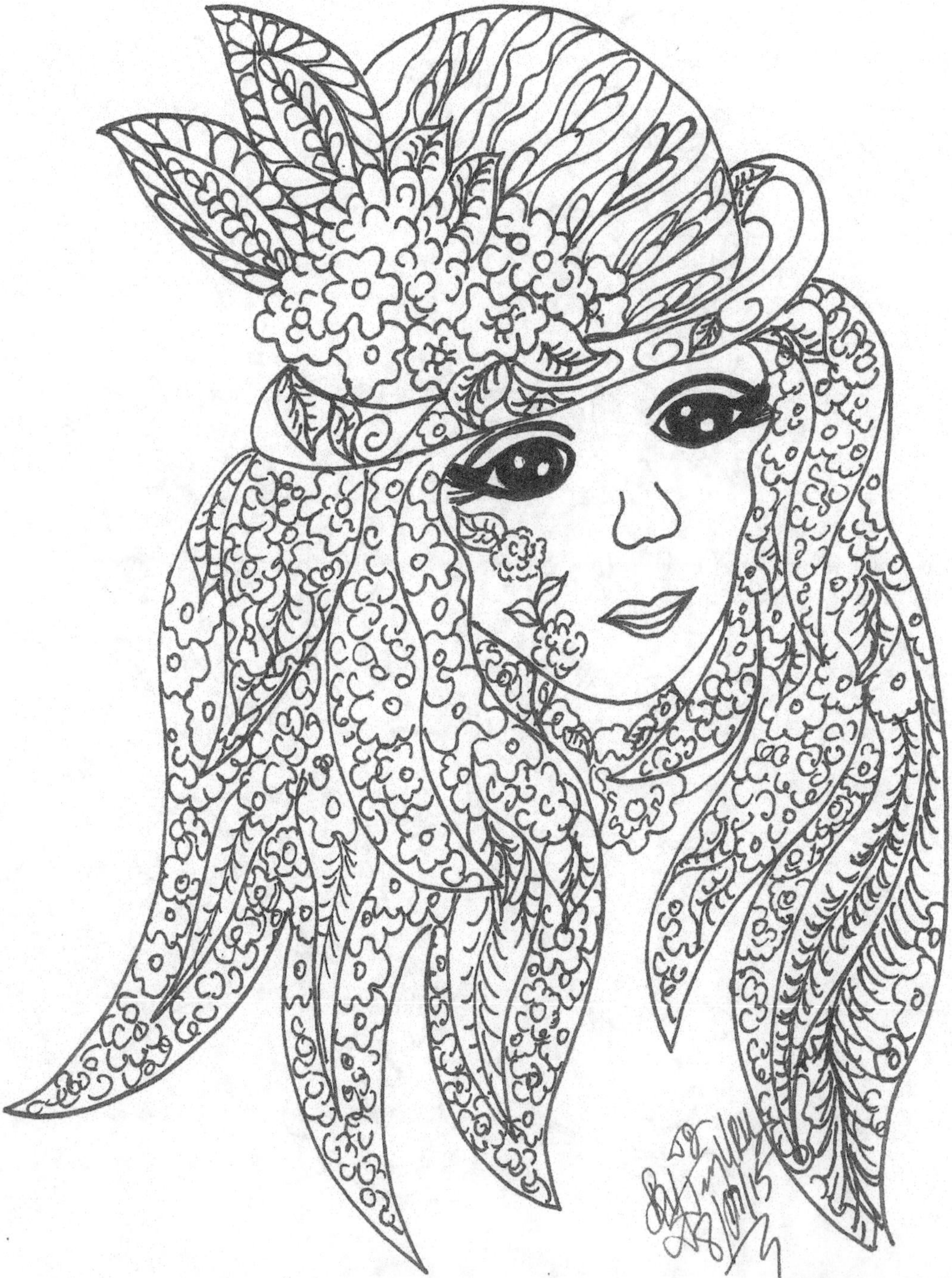

www.ingramcontent.com/pod-product-compliance
Lightning Source LLC
Chambersburg PA
CBHW080626180526
45168CB00007B/3076